The Top 10 Habits of Underachievers

By Andre C. Hatchett

Dedication:

There are many people who have had a profound impact on my personal and professional development. I would like to thank my big, big brother, Leader Warren Hatchett. He is a fantastic example of adulthood and fatherhood. He leads not just by his words, but by his example.

I'd also like to thank Leader Lex Kelly. Lex is a young brother who uses his platform and his influence to empower others. He is a top-notch friend with an amazing soul.

There are people who come into our lives who leave indelible imprints. Leader Temitayo Osinubi is one of those people. I want to thank him for his "never die" attitude, his consistent friendship and his unwavering support.

Lastly, I want to thank those of you who are reading this book and who have supported me. I love you all!

The Top 10 Habits of Underachievers

Table of Contents

Introduction: "Underachiever"

"Underachiever" is a word that many of us don't like to hear. Who wants to admit that they are not working up to their potential? Unfortunately, there are many people who fall into this category. After being one, befriending some, and studying other underachievers, I've realized that most of them had certain traits in common, even if they didn't know each other.

This tells me that there are habits that make one more inclined to underachieve. As someone who looks for solutions, I realized that it's scary to see people underachieving with such frequency. So, I started watching them more carefully with a keen eye. I wanted to know what did they do? How did they do it? And, more importantly, what didn't they do?

As a master encourager and motivator, my goal is to help people operate to their fullest potential. I take it personally when I can't help people achieve their goals. It is for this reason that I wrote this book. It is not enough that I noticed these habits and traits; my purpose is to help do something about it. By making people aware through a book, it is something that they can pick up over and over again. It is true that sometimes giving someone your words is more impactful than telling them.

And let's be honest. The word underachiever is harsh. Trust me, I know. However, I want to be clear that this is not about blaming or antagonizing. This is about being our best selves. When I use this word, I am not judging you by society's standards. My standard is that YOU should never accept a lesser version of you!! Perhaps you have suppressed yourself or dimmed your light so others could shine. Indeed, it is likely that part of you is alive while another part of you is dying. Once you tackle and dismantle that inner underachiever in you then you start to actually live. This book is about showing you how.

1. They live in the past.

Many underachievers have a tendency to walk forward while looking backwards. They emphasize what they could have done. They also talk ALOT about they should have done. Some may proudly brag about who they could have dated and what they could have earned. The truth is that the time that they've put into thinking about the past, could have been time and energy put into the present and actually making true strides. Unfortunately, when you ignore the present and the future, you are stuck in the past. The next time that you drive down, "Live in the past lane," LOUDLY YELL AT YOURSELF TO STOP!!! Also, stop telling your friends this crap. It's OVER!!! Be intentional about not coming across as bitter. Remember, overachievers, don't spend time with bitter people.

NOTES

2. They master overthinking.

Perfection is the enemy of execution. -Evan Carmichael

This topic could be an ENTIRE book by itself, so imagine this scenario:

"Andre, I have this idea."

"Great, let me hear it."

[Two weeks later] "How's your thing coming along?"

"Oh, I was talking to my (loser) friends. And they told me it wouldn't work so, I gave up (the way you always do)."

Unfortunately, this happens more often than not. My question is: Why didn't you follow through? For many, the addiction to overthinking is killing them while they're still alive. Please, please stop it! How do you change this?

It takes 2 steps:

Step 1—You have to ignore the end results and block them out. It is tempting to say, "She's hot and has a great bod." But, don't think about marrying her after your first encounter. Instead, you should focus on saying *hello* and getting her phone number. That's it. Take it one step at a time with great intentionality. The key is action. Yes, you need to think (but not too much).

Step 2—Hire an accountability partner. Pay someone to watch you or sit with you. Have that person stay on the phone with you while you work on the task at hand. They might not even have to talk. They just need to be there. Consequently, there is a greater likelihood that you will achieve your plans (not goals, but PLANS) and that your productivity will increase by 79%. Notice that I didn't say join a Facebook group. Virtual communities serve a purpose, but the real results are derived when you pay money to an accountability coach. For example, you can go to AndreCHatchett.com to hire me.

NOTES

3. They are addicted to comfort.

They aren't happy. In many instances, underachievers aren't making enough money. However, they won't change. They say things like, "This is what I've always done." Personally, I'm not sure about that. Greatness is often born out of discomfort. Underachievers tend to allow the fucking evil comfort to step back in. Yes, I said you allow it. If your success requires you to do something new, do it! Move to a different country or state. Travel to far-away places. Learn technology and do something innovative.

NOTES

4. They date other underachievers.

Say this with me, especially the ladies: *I am who I date.* Say it a little louder for the ninjas in the back: *I am who I date.* PERIOD!

So, when you say I only date and attract losers, you are saying that's who you are. Ironically, there are pros for dating an underachiever.

1. They won't push you.
2. They will allow you to be your least self.
3. They're easier to control.

Thankfully, there are antidotes. How do you date overachievers? You take steps.

1. Exercise at least 3 days a week.
2. Become an expert in a particular field and get paid for it.

3. Go to where they are and start with *hello*. Make it clear that you are there to win. Winners value and appreciate other winners.

NOTES

5. They lack discipline.

"Hey Dre, what are you doing today?"

"Since we went out the last two nights, today, I'm working late."

"Hey Dre, I just closed a deal."

"Great! I'm happy for you! Want to go to happy hour? My treat?"

"Shouldn't you invest or save that money?"

"Nah man, I need a drink and Marshalls has a sale (they always have sales—it's Marshalls)."

So, as you are thinking about this exchange, think about what's being valued. Many underachievers live for the moment and for the weekend. They need their joy *now*. So, they don't save that 3.5% it takes for a down payment to buy that $100,000 condo (that will appreciate to$225,000).

Stop buying new clothes—you don't really need to go to Marshalls. Avoid going to happy hour four times a week for 6 months. If you must go, go twice a week. The point is that money adds up. You will be amazed at what you *can* afford. If you had saved the down payment money of $3,500, you could have made $125,000 on the sale of that condo. But, you needed the immediate gratification. Give delayed gratification a try—it will pay off!

NOTES

6. They take shortcuts.

Underachievers have an addiction to looking for an easy way in and out. It's a frame of mind. It's a lifestyle. The reality is that it is who they have been allowed to become. Is it all about working harder and harder? Sure, that works at times. But taking shortcuts, no matter how hard you work, will backfire. For example, when you start missing details repeatedly, you're done. I have developed a reputation as an excellent instructor. Is this because I am super-duper smart or because I spell everything correctly? Nope. It is because I have an ability to take complex formulas and simplify them so that a 14-year-old and a Ph.D. gets what I am saying.

I also offer bonus classes to make sure that they get it. See, I go the extra mile. I make sure my point is made in an effective manner and that my students understand me. I don't assume that they d0; I make sure that they do. You cannot take shortcuts and go the extra mile. 92% of the people won't do this. Over time, your reputation will spread—fast, far, and long. The question is: Is it worth it?

NOTES

7. They don't assess, screen & upgrade their friends.

Screen your friends like you're an overprotective Dad and your teenage daughter is going on her first date. They must bring value to you. And you must do the same for them. If it helps, place them in one of these categories:

1. After work drinking buddies
2. Emotionally supportive friends
3. Push me to my goals friends
4. Partnership friends—we work on deals together
5. Sunday brunch friends

Then breakdown how often you talk with them and why.

I spent YEARS trying to convince some of my friends of their greatness. Fuck it, I tried showing them their above averageness. We would talk, get hyped, and nothing would happen. I later categorized these friends as great humans, but not overly productive friends. When I have similar talks with my great-hearted people/overachiever friends, things get done. The quality of my conversations hasn't changed, but whom I am having them with has! This has led to a different output.

NOTES

8. They lack focus.

Most of us have difficulty focusing, but we don't hire people to help us focus. Yes, it may seem odd to hire someone to help you do something that should come naturally. Trust me, having an accountability coach can make you millions of dollars. Try this exercise to understand my point: Write down every time you log into Instagram and how long you logged in for. Do the same thing for Facebook and Twitter. Write down what you did on these platforms and for EXACTLY how long. You liked Amber Rose's pictures or maybe you have a new friend request. I am going to keep the solution simple:

Delete the apps.

NOTES

9. They have too many goals and not enough plans.

When you talk to some underachievers, they sound great. They get very excited, but the goals stop right there. Even in their loud voices, the excitement wears off. I used to be that guy. However, I changed it. I learned to shut up! I, then, released my mouth when I had PayPal links and log-ins. My point here is that I stopped talking until I had things lined up and ready to launch. They were in motion. I could point to something and say, look here. Order here. I became a closer and not a big talker. I GOT THINGS DONE! Now, I respect myself a lot more than I used to. I get high off of advancing others to this point. Simply put, become a doer!

NOTES

10. They have an inferiority complex.

You will never out earn, out date, or out-perform your belief system. For example, I had a friend who was in a rut. He sold some products that earned him some profit! Win!!! Then, he got excited. However, he stopped promoting that product.

Weird, right? He became upset with his money status because he made money and then he stopped doing what did to earn the money in the first place.

When you suffer from an insecurity, you resort back to how you think of yourself. It's sad to watch.

How do you overcome this? When something works, KEEP DOING IT!!! It's working. Block out the rest of the crap in your overloaded head. Remember, you are superior!!

NOTES

11. They just don't want it.

You know what, that's fine. I mean it. It's cool. If you truly believe that there is nothing wrong with being an underachiever or being average and you don't want more, life will proceed as normal for you. For those of you who realize that underachieving is not what you want, life is torturous. You will be in a constant state of turmoil and experience internal chaos.

I strive to be an overachiever; it takes everything inside of me and more. When I even have a thought about averageness, I get disgusted with myself. I'm not made for average. Not an average day, sex, queen or life. I'm here to kick ass and take names. I am typing this book at 8:07 pm EST on a Sunday night. There is a Deep House party at a Black owned pub by my office. The rum punch there is mean! I want to go—really bad! But you need this book and I need to write it for you. See, I need this!

I don't need the party. That's why underachieving won't work for me, and it never will. Advancement for me is addictive. The sale isn't. The party is cool, but not as cool as telling a lady, "I just wrote my second book." *Scarface.*

NOTES

How do you change these patterns?

You have to see these as habits and all habits can change. Here's my personal breakdown about making that shift. To replace a bad habit, you must have a good one. It's easier for most people to replace physical habits than mental ones, but both are achievable.

Should you consider yourself an overachiever or just an achiever?

It all starts with a need. Keep in mind that 'wants' don't get the work done, but 'needs' do. So, for me, personally, I NEEDED to be around Black people who were out earning me and who were doing more impactful work than I was doing in the community. So, I wrote their names down on a list—a couple of them were Dr. Boyce Watkins and Jay "Mr. Real Estate" Morrison.

That was in 2012. Now in 2017, I have friendships and working relationships with both of these icons.

It was a need! I volunteered. I interned. I *offered first* and then asked on the backend.

1. I stopped trying to save dead people.

This may be hard, but let go of people who you have spoken with about a problem, but who refuse to listen. If you gave them sound advice and they have chosen not to act on it then you have done your part—move on.

NOTES

2. I offer better quality work, products, or services.

I shot professional commercials—expressive ones for me at the time. This showed the world and potential partners, clients, and customers that I was the real deal. When your online presence is solid, you do less convincing. I also spent a $1,000 on my personal website: AndreCHatchett.com

NOTES

3. I became known as a consistent person.

I am not perfect, but I showed up and did above average work. Period. Having the reputation as an above average and the consistent person is better than a person who is known for very good or even great work, especially if they are unreliable.

NOTES

4. I left the State of NY fulltime.

I needed some damn perspective. Note that I said NEEDED. I didn't like saying that I've always lived in NY. I needed to stretch myself and expand my brain. For the past two years, I have spent about 3 months in Dallas, TX and Atlanta, GA. I am no longer a lifelong New Yorker.

NOTES

5. I made fewer obligations to people.

I started charging for mentoring and consultations. I say "no" and or, "I'll let you know at a later date." Over commitments were killing my focus and mentally weighing me down. I had to change that and it worked.

NOTES

6. I took a year and ½ off from serious dating.

I wanted to date top-quality women and I wanted them to take me seriously. So, I had to take time off from dating. I developed myself from the inside out. And then I stepped back on the scene. And it worked! Most people won't do this. They think they need someone else all of the time, even someone they don't like or respect. Not me—I understand the value of delayed gratification.

NOTES

7. I hired two assistants with better skill sets.

Once I was forced to accept that one of my major issues was overloading myself, I hired consistent help. I hire them on an *as needed* basis. This was one of my most strategic moves to date! My addiction to overloading myself was costing me thousands of dollars a year and it was stressing me out.

The ability to assign a task to someone else allows you to focus on bigger things that you can tackle yourself. I am so glad that I matured in this area— so glad! Here's a quick example: I was charged a penalty of $724.00 for not handing in some tax documents on time. If I would have had an assistant in place, my assistant would have taken care of filling the taxes or, at least, making sure that I had applied for an extension. So not spending the $12.00- $24.00 actually cost me $724.00.

NOTES

8. I upgraded my environments.

I have an office at a co-working space now and a membership at one of the best gyms in the country. This puts me where I NEED to be. The office is open, clean, warm and organized. I am happy when I go there. The people I am around are doing amazing things. And it is worth noting that the gym has one of the best steam rooms and showers I have ever experienced. All of this is to say that I had to change my surroundings.

NOTES

9. I dry clean my clothing. A huge time saver.

Think about how much money and time you spent on dry cleaning. Don't believe me? Go get all of your receipts from the last two months. How much did you spend?

NOTES

10. I do the free stuff like I'm getting paid big bucks to do it.

This is HUGE. You would never know the difference in my pay between one event and another because I am going to bring the heat regardless! If I say I am giving you a ride to the airport, I am on time and beaming with a smile. If I start a limo service and you hire me at $400.0 an hour to take you to the airport, I am on time with a smile!

NOTES

11. I over act and under think.

The old adage, "Actions speak louder than words [and thoughts] is appropriate. Sometimes, we have a tendency to think about things more than we actually do them. This leads to a lot of wasted time. Remember, there are a lot of things that you can get back in life and time is NOT one of them.

NOTES

12. I stopped forming alliances with other complicated people.

Complicated people can be some of the most difficult people to deal with—they are often complicated for reasons. On the surface, this may be alluring and appealing, but you may find that it takes a lot of time and energy trying to convince them to do things. In some instances, simplicity is best.

NOTES

13. I believe in affirmations.

Talking myself into my higher self is a daily ritual. Listening to thousands of hours of videos and audio books about overcoming adversity have changed my mindset. I think about hard work, and being a billionaire. Overloading my brain with positive things has created a new and MAXIMIZING belief system!

In conclusion, I hope that the ease of clarity and simplicity of expression will enable this book to help you. None of us are destined to be underachievers.

NOTES

Next Steps

Now that you have read the book from beginning to end, I want you to do one of these things:

1. Be aware of what makes someone an underachiever.

2. Be disgusted with yourself if you are an underachiever. Get mad and take some action!! You can turn the corner and change.

3. Give this book to someone who should be operating at a higher level. You may see it and they may talk it. For every problem, there is a solution. This book just might be what they need to become an overachiever!

Until our paths across again, I thank you for reading this book!

NOTES

NOTES

NOTES

NOTES

About the Author

Andre C. Hatchett is a nationally acclaimed entrepreneur and philanthropist. As the current owner of TheBlackRealEstateSchool.com, AndresNotarySchool.com and Priority Notary, Inc., Andre is a man who wears many successful hats.

Andre is the driving force behind the national Black Business Challenge social media campaign that encourages African-Americans to patronize businesses owned and operated by black entrepreneurs.

Andre attributes his passion and entrepreneurial drive to his father who taught him, "If you go to school with someone, you should never have to work for them." Those profound words resonated with Andre at a young age. Before high school, Andre shoveled snow, sold lemonade, and wholesaled candy. His entrepreneurial skills positioned him for success as he transitioned from boyhood to manhood.

At the age of 22, Andre completed the formidable task of being a first-time homeowner. Without letting any dust settle, he then purchased a second home at the young age of 23. Continuing his real estate success, he has worked as a Business Consultant, Professional Coach, and currently he serves as a skilled Real Estate Sales Expert, earning him the nickname "Mr. Condo."

He is also the founder of the Own or Be Owned movement which includes the thought-provoking and insightful book, Own or Be Owned – The Black Man's Guide To Wealth Creation in America. In addition, Andre owns a clothing line: ClothingBuyBlack.com. A brilliant entrepreneur, Andre is often called upon to share his knowledge with others. He can be seen in the the up and coming documentary Own or Be Owned. Remember, home values will go up with or without you!

Made in the USA
Middletown, DE
13 April 2021

37552065R00044